~ Poems, Folklore, History, Images ~

Bill Boudreau
~ 2012 ~

WEDGEPORT – Bill Boudreau
~ Poems, Folklore, History, Images ~

Contents

Acknowledgement 4
Preface and Dedication 5
Echafauds de Pré (back then)...6
Hill of the Cross (*Butte d'la Croix*) 7
Mon Village (a song) 9
Wedgeport, Acadia 11
Renaissance (today) 13
Breakwater Wharf 14
Wedgeport 16
Saint Michael Church 17
Harris Island 19
Irish Moss 20
Worm Digging 21
Drying Cod *(morue sec)* 23
Marsh Hay *(Foin Salé)* 24
Winters 26
Mark of the Villagers 28
Speck' Island (folklore) 29
Saint Marton – Big Tusket Island 30
Massacre Island (folklore) 31
Stranger from the Sea (folklore) 32
Wilson Island (folklore) 33
Dead Body – *Corp Mort* (folklore) 34
Legend of the Rappie Pie (*L'Ordre du Bon Temps*) 35
Blue Fin (a song) 38
Pêcheur de Hier (a song) 39
The Gate (a ballad) 41
Atlantic Ocean 43
L'Hetriere 45
Acadians 46
1755 (a song – English version) 47
1755 (a song – French version) 49

WEDGEPORT – Bill Boudreau
~ Poems, Folklore, History, Images ~

~ Images ~ 51
Off to Conquer the Atlantic Ocean 52
Marais – Canals 52
Sun and Fog embrace Saint Michael church 53
A clear day in Wedgeport 53
Fruits de Mer 54
Repose 55
Ready for the Deep 55
Tusket Islands 56
St. Marton Island looking toward Harris Island 56
Deep Cove 57
Pussy Willow 57
Scallop Haul 58
Jules Pothier's, Pierre Boudreau's Houses, and Wedgeport Inn 58
Big Halibut 59
Close Up 60
Herring Load 61
Tuna Wharf Museum 61
Vive L'Acadie 62
Expulsion – a 1755 Tragedy 63
About the Author 72

WEDGEPORT – Bill Boudreau
~ Poems, Folklore, History, Images ~

Acknowledgement

A couple of years ago when I joined Facebook (fb), I began making friends with people from Wedgeport. I quickly saw that they were posting beautiful Wedgeport photos. I saved them on my computer. These photos give me pleasure and excite reminisces of my time in Wedgeport.

What I didn't do, however, was associate the photos with the fb friend. I regret that now. If any of my fb friends sees his or her photos in the book, please accept my gratitude for giving me the opportunity to share images of Wedgeport to the world.

WEDGEPORT – Bill Boudreau
~ Poems, Folklore, History, Images ~

Preface and Dedication

These poems and ballads document memories of where I grew up and images of the past and present. The verses and images depict places, people, legends, and historical events pertaining to Wedgeport and surroundings.

To add a touch of realism, I've used Wedgeport *patois* spoken words. I have spelled these words as daily pronounced, for example, "cha" for quai, "Cha du Douca," for Quai des Doucette, etc. At times, I've used my imagination to dramatize incidents, situations, or personalities. But the fundamental idea has its roots in the Wedgeport culture.

I have taken pieces of our Acadian history and known personalities from different time periods to represent events and make the poem or ballad more interesting, such as, "Legend of the Rappie Pie," where people from the present and the past interact in a fictitious setting.

On a personal note, growing up in Wedgeport gave me a foundation and a set of values to build on and survive the intensely competitive world. To this day, decades later, since I left Wedgeport, these values still serve as my beacon.

And finally, I dedicate this book to the Wedgeport people, from the founders to those living today, because we created these verses by being ourselves. As the writer, born and raised in Wedgeport, I merely report who we are. I realize more than ever that we are unique and special in more ways than we know.

WEDGEPORT – Bill Boudreau
~ Poems, Folklore, History, Images ~

Echafauds de Pré (back then)

As summer seasons past over
Mounds scattered the marshlands
Monuments of a fading culture
New tide slowly covered the land

WEDGEPORT – Bill Boudreau
~ Poems, Folklore, History, Images ~

Hill of the Cross (*Butte d'la Croix*)

Years of wander
A longing to be free
Hill by Tusket River
Prayers to the Lord
A cross in the earth
Wedgeport's birth

WEDGEPORT – Bill Boudreau
~ Poems, Folklore, History, Images ~

On a hill in Wedgeport, a simple wooden cross commemorates the first mass held in 1769 for the returning Acadians. The Hill of the Cross (Butte d'la Croix) remains a symbol of Acadian courage and perseverance. The site also features a saltmarsh boardwalk and a magnificent view of the Tusket River and Tusket Islands.

WEDGEPORT – Bill Boudreau
~ Poems, Folklore, History, Images ~

Mon Village (a song)

*Les colons a la Butte d'a Croix
Église majestueuse de Ste. Michel
Les esprits des pêchers moyer
La grande mer entre terre et ciel*

*Refrain:
Ca c'est Mon Village
La source de mon pouvoir
Ou j'etet enfant
Tousjour ma profond gloire*

*Les bâtiments du temp passé
La pêche mondial au gros thon
Le foin salé sur les prés
Père et garçon dan leur bateau
(Refrain)*

WEDGEPORT – Bill Boudreau
~ Poems, Folklore, History, Images ~

L'Étoile dors de l'Acadie
La rivière bleu qui nous guide
Pointe de terre avec des isles
Sur l'ocean les pêchers navige
(Refrain)
Un mille sept cents soixante-sept
L'année de notre fondation
Deux cents vingt-cinq ans plus tard
On cri de celebration
(Refrain)

WEDGEPORT – Bill Boudreau
~ Poems, Folklore, History, Images ~

Wedgeport, Acadia

A strip of land with rocky shores
From mainland between ocean water
Southern tip, visible islands and shoals
Some bare, others sheltered

Eastern view across waterway
Tusket River at down of day
Dique's trees and sunlight meet
At sunset, *Grand Bois'* silhouette

Twice a day, massive tide
Bare mudflats it hides
Spring to midsummer
Perennial fog a cover

Village engulfed in mist
Damp and chill to the bone
Weeks on end, no sun
As if sky was undone

On foggy days inhabitants hear
Mournful call of the foghorn
Warning boats, danger near
Prayers for sun to reappear

Chas on rocky coast
In degrees of utility
Some, in time decayed
Others in operability

WEDGEPORT – Bill Boudreau
~ Poems, Folklore, History, Images ~

South, first on the west
Di-Cha, a pile of squared rocks
Held together by vertical poles
Runners holding bolder blocks

Bay channel for boats to follow
Leads to *Di-Cha* at tide low
Two or three boats tied to it
No more can fit

Along west coast, going south
One arrives at *Cha du Douca*
Point of commercial fishing
Channel poles guide boats in

String of boats along *Chas*
Several anchored off shore
Few on land, getting ready
All at different readiness

Cha du Douca, fish for sale
Unloaded and mechanically conveyed
To factory for gutting and fillet
Women hand cleaning fish in bale

Further south is Tuna Wharf
Glimmer of grander from the past
Giant Blue Fins made other fish dwarfs
Tournament once held in class

Tuna Wharf's great days are gone by
I vividly remember as child
Hooked on Rip, landed on dock
Giant Blue Fins scaffolded in flock

WEDGEPORT – Bill Boudreau
~ Poems, Folklore, History, Images ~

World team anglers
From many nations
Each believed had omen
For days, competition heralded

Renaissance (today)

Sport Tuna Fishing Museum and Interpretive Center

WEDGEPORT – Bill Boudreau
~ Poems, Folklore, History, Images ~

Breakwater Wharf

South, east coast, mouth of Tusket River
More exposed to Atlantic Ocean
Boats afloat, sea wide open
Breakwater Wharf's enclosure blocks high water

In days of hurricane storm
Waves hit Breakwater Wharf's wall
Ocean force before sea falls
Nature's energy in top form

Inland, along north shore
Entrance to the Cape Bay
In small cove, sheltered like a fort
Cha-á -Charlie for locals to take

WEDGEPORT – Bill Boudreau
~ Poems, Folklore, History, Images ~

In the bay passing between
Cha-a-Charlie and *Cha-du-Chebec*
Once proud ships docked, now serene
Skeletal remains of days so great

It's been said that great sail ships
In multitude docked here in slips
Load fish and sail to South Seas
Brothers carelessly fell to their knees

Cha-du-Nord, well in Cape Bay
Sheltered between Cape and Islet
Serves fishermen down that way
All fishermen's need well kept

WEDGEPORT – Bill Boudreau
~ Poems, Folklore, History, Images ~

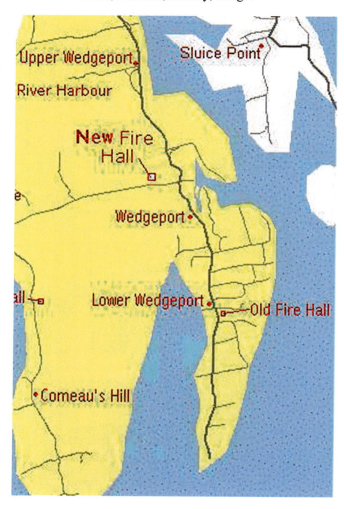

Wedgeport

Village, a finger of land
Leading to point of rocky shoreline
From mainland with bushes and trees
Main road thru village, five miles

WEDGEPORT – Bill Boudreau
~ Poems, Folklore, History, Images ~

Saint Michael Church

Midway, church proud and mystique
Two steeples, white, tall, and still
Demands worship from the Catholics
Dominates village from the hill

Two thousands or so inhabitants
Majority are fishermen
Herring, lobster, or cod, whatever the season
Salted blood, ocean schooled

WEDGEPORT – Bill Boudreau
~ Poems, Folklore, History, Images ~

On ocean they ventured
Pushing to catch their measures
Rough seas and storms their enemy
Nor'easter feared terribly

WEDGEPORT – Bill Boudreau
~ Poems, Folklore, History, Images ~

Harris Island

Temporary base for lobster fishing
Shanties lined in rows
Winter weeks, share shanty
Hired cook, hard working men, home to many

Chas, tall on barnacle poles in water
Covered with rows of lobster traps
Piles of buoys with owners' mark in color
Boats tide afloat, rope tied with slack

WEDGEPORT – Bill Boudreau
~ Poems, Folklore, History, Images ~

Irish Moss

Twice a day at low tide, Irish Mossing
In dory with heavy rack, back breaking
Rocky shoals, moss on rocks like hide
Racking in wind, sea current, and tide

Irish moss spread on side of roads
For drying to crisp before sacking
Wish for bright sun before selling
Extended fog makes moss mold

WEDGEPORT – Bill Boudreau
~ Poems, Folklore, History, Images ~

Worm Digging

Low tide on mud flats, ankle deep
With four-prong pick digging, a tough feat
Back bend and arms in steady motion
Worms pulled from bottom of ocean

WEDGEPORT – Bill Boudreau
~ Poems, Folklore, History, Images ~

Sea worms, long and slimy
Out of the mud stretch two feet
Large head in fore skin, hidden beak
Pale yellow, soft flesh, break easy

Disturbed mud flats at low tide
Sea covers as ocean rise
Sell worm, penny a piece
For bait, not to keep

WEDGEPORT – Bill Boudreau
~ Poems, Folklore, History, Images ~

Drying Cod *(Morue Sec)*

Cod fish cleaned, soaked in brine
Opened flat on wooden benches
Long spread on side of roads
To sun-dry before stored

Dry hard cod ready stored in cellar
De-salted and boiled with vegetables
Salt fish dinners, meat replacement
Source of food for the winter

WEDGEPORT – Bill Boudreau
~ Poems, Folklore, History, Images ~

Marsh Hay *(Foin Salé)*

Spring and Summer
Preparation for long winter
Low tide, on marshland
Salt Hay cut with scythe in hand

Spread in sun to dry
Hay racked in rows
Before lumped in piles
Ready for *pré echafauds*

Like ancient ruins, *pré echafauds*
Spread across marsh flats
Sea beaten posts stuck in the ground
Old wood boards on top for platform

WEDGEPORT – Bill Boudreau
~ Poems, Folklore, History, Images ~

On soft earth, salt hay piles
Two poles slid under *barge*
Lifted off the ground
Two men carry with *Tien Barge*

Carry piles to *pré echafauds*
Mounds of salt hay
On poles, protected from tide
Weights on top, hay not fly away

Salt hay *barge* on marshes
Coming of Fall
Fresh hay already in barn
Long winter, feed for cows

WEDGEPORT – Bill Boudreau
~ Poems, Folklore, History, Images ~

Winters

Winters, cold and wet
Ground, a mix of fog and snow
Slush would freeze toes
Enduring the long stretch

WEDGEPORT – Bill Boudreau
~ Poems, Folklore, History, Images ~

Three in a bed and four blankets
Pot belly stove to warm the house
Lighted coal would soon burn out
Dawn, visible breath, windows sealed in ice

In long johns with butt flap
Heavy woolen knitted socks in feet
Dress quickly, run to outhouse for crap
Before a warm bowl of cream of wheat

Arrival of winter
Vegetables in cellar
Barrels of brine and fish
For winter, the main dish

WEDGEPORT – Bill Boudreau
~ Poems, Folklore, History, Images ~

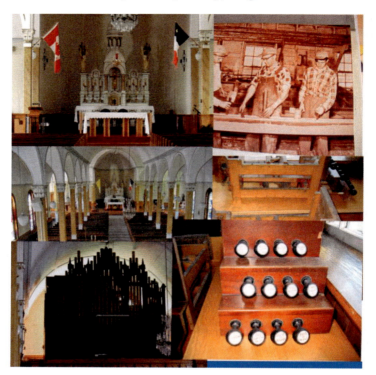

Mark of the Villagers

With love of craft and skilled hands
Carved the village, houses, and land
Built ocean faring fishing boats
For rough seas and staying afloat
Crafted artistic pulpit and pews
From which they listened to the Word
Sadly with time and new views
Mark of their work replaced
With cold, modern commercial face
Loss of respect for the work of ancestors

WEDGEPORT – Bill Boudreau
~ Poems, Folklore, History, Images ~

Speck' Island (folklore)

Speck', a far off island
Bare, no trees and vulnerable
To the cold Atlantic and wind
In cove, to few fishermen, bearable

This desolate remote place we're told
Place of many shipwrecks long ago
What stories does it hold?
Erased by nature's anger, nobody knows

On winter nights, passing of storms
Wandering on cold seashore
A headless man walking alone
Searching, it's not known what for

A story that's been retold
Generation to generation
Believed by Speck's fishermen
Never to disturb the night so cold

WEDGEPORT – Bill Boudreau
~ Poems, Folklore, History, Images ~

Saint Marton – Big Tusket Island

Shells on *Saint Marton's* seashore
Variety of shapes and colors
What stories do they tell?
Of ocean bottom horrors

From shore, washed every day
Back into the ocean to sway
With tides and waves floating
To Harris Island across the way

WEDGEPORT – Bill Boudreau
~ Poems, Folklore, History, Images ~

Massacre Island (folklore)

Massacre Island, it's been told
In pioneers days, a massacre did unfold
On this island lived a peaceful tribe
Attack upon them came as surprise

Pirates came to island
Massacred all inhabitants
Peaceful, had no defense implements
Blood flowed from every child, man and woman

WEDGEPORT – Bill Boudreau
~ Poems, Folklore, History, Images ~

Stranger from the Sea (folklore)

Engulfed by the cold Atlantic Sea
Wedgeport surroundings carry a history
From early sixteen hundredths
War among English, French, and pirates

Stories of the past have been told
Of strange happenings of old
Sightings of mysterious ships
Out and in the fog swift

It's been said that an unknown ship
In a sea cove up the bay
Seen by villagers at end of day
In the fog it sailed away

In the morning on the reef
A desperate man was found
Cut off were his arms
And no legs for his feet

Caring and compassionate the village
The stranger was taken in
Sounds he made, not a known language
Food and warmth were offered him

Cared for as one of their own
Never know, what land his home
Linguist from far away came
Listened, never knew his name

He died a mysterious man
His passing is in our lives
As the sea carries over the miles
Mysterious tales of faraway lands

WEDGEPORT – Bill Boudreau
~ Poems, Folklore, History, Images ~

Wilson Island (folklore)

Wilson Island so the story goes
Was named for a snoopy nose
In days of pirates of old
Island was their temporary home

Wilson, a man who was nosy
Rowed to the island in his dory
There is no more to the story
Pirates sent Wilson to his glory

WEDGEPORT – Bill Boudreau
~ Poems, Folklore, History, Images ~

Dead Body – *Corp Mort* (folklore)

Dead Body, *Corp Mort*, a spot of rocks
At the mouth of the Tusket River
Unknown burial with erected cross
Grave used by fishermen as marker

Mysteriously, the cross would fall
No matter how firmly
A passing fisherman would make it tall
Next day, not straight at all

Speculated by old fishermen
The mystery of falling cross
A buried corpse sends a warning
Be careful near these rocks

WEDGEPORT – Bill Boudreau
~ Poems, Folklore, History, Images ~

Legend of the Rappie Pie (*L'Ordre du Bon Temps*)

In early sixteen hundredths
Colonial Acadians in desperate times
Long cold winters and short of food
Needed event to brighten mood

Champlain introduced "Order of Good Time"
A get together of all people
Removed misery from their minds
Sharing potatoes, chicken, and pork if able

WEDGEPORT – Bill Boudreau
~ Poems, Folklore, History, Images ~

Large quantity of food in preparation
Sharing the work before dancing
Peeling and grading potatoes, then squeezing
In cloth bags, starch out in filtration

On stove, large pots of boiling chicken
Little pieces of chopped onions
Pork chunks for good greasing
Boiling water, getting ready for the mixing

Large pans with dry graded potatoes
Boiling chicken broth poured on top
With large wooden spoon stirring
Until liquid is evenly gobbled up

Process continued with boiling water
Stirring to get to an even matter
A thick grayest sauce mash
Ready for the pan, with salt and pepper

Melted butter in heated pan
Pour mash and spread with hand
A layer of chicken and pork pieces
Before pouring the rest in pan

A few chucks of butter on top
Large pan filled even to the rim
Into the oven for long time cooking
Clean dishes, everyone feeling prim

Andrew á Charlie got his fiddle
Joe á Andrew picked up his banjo
Melvin á Andrew fetched his accordion
The crowd was ready to go

WEDGEPORT – Bill Boudreau
~ Poems, Folklore, History, Images ~

The music picked up beat
Young and old with tapping feet
Lines formed, movement to and fro
Swinging partners, do-si-do

Acadians in joyful height
Father Sigogne admiring the sight
Bénoit á 'ti Pius brought the brew
A potent mix everyone knew

Happy, they dance and sang
Until a late hour rang
The smell was appetizing
While Rappie Pie was cooking

Tired, dancing no longer able
At tables, they all sat on chairs
Elders and priest at head table
Father Sigogne recited a prayer

They ate their fill of Rappie Pie
For dessert, home cooked apple pie
Fresh milk from their cows
For the elders, some dandelion wine

Happiness by sharing was gotten
For some few hours the evening
The cold winter was forgotten
Returning home joyful and singing

So, out of the "Order of Good Time"
Came the traditional Rappie Pie
More than three hundred years past
The Acadians still make it last!

WEDGEPORT – Bill Boudreau
~ Poems, Folklore, History, Images ~

Blue Fin (a song)

Many years ago in boats afloat
On the Rip it was a great sport
Giant tuna fish caught for fun
By the hundreds at day's done

The Blue Fin was a beautiful fish
At high speed on the ocean swells
Tuna and sea in perfect harmony
In schools, swam so very well

Anglers cursed from the pulpit
Word of the prophet came to be
Blue Fin vanished from the sea
No more Blue Fins there to see

WEDGEPORT – Bill Boudreau
~ Poems, Folklore, History, Images ~

Pêcheur de Hier (a song)

Toi le Pêcheur de Hier
Té parti vers les isles
Pour fair pêche sur la mer
On t'attend sur la rive

Refrain:
On regard vers l'ocean
On t'appel pour secours
Tu navigue un voyage
Qui n'a pas de retour

Tu guide le jeune pecheur
Quand perdu dans la brume
Les houles dit ton passé
On va pas ton oublier

(Refrain)

At toi on fait homage
Tes parti de notre vu
Le vent port ton message
Les thons son disparu

(Refrain)

WEDGEPORT – Bill Boudreau
~ Poems, Folklore, History, Images ~

The Gate (a ballad)

Alone he went on his way
Left for west of the Rip
At dawn on a foggy day
His return was a weary night
The sea was rolling high
There were no lights in sight
In the wind he heard a cry

> Whooooo …
> Whooooo…

The storm roared as it rose
He rowed toward the Gate
As he thought of his mistakes
But it was much too late

> Whooooo …
> Whooooo…

WEDGEPORT – Bill Boudreau
~ Poems, Folklore, History, Images ~

As he approached the edge
Saw a glow on the ledge
A fisherman dressed in white
Shouting cries in the night

    Whooooo …
    Whooooo…

Wanted to save stranded soul
He sailed to the Gate's shoal
He heard the word too late
Got shipwrecked at the Gate

    Whooooo …
    Whooooo…

Eternity, the fisherman's fate (spoken)

    Whooooo …
    Whooooo…

    Whooooo …
    Whooooo…

WEDGEPORT – Bill Boudreau
~ Poems, Folklore, History, Images ~

Atlantic Ocean

Strong, mighty, and dominant
Deep, endless, meets firmament
Giver of life, taker of life
On earth, no force can fight

WEDGEPORT – Bill Boudreau
~ Poems, Folklore, History, Images ~

Gentle, soothing provider
Cradle of life, battlefield of death
Living things must surrender
Violent power, without fret

Master of human race
Unpredictable, uneasy to face
Enormous energy stored in grace
Only the sky can embrace

Little understanding, we respect
Without warning, can be a threat
Shades of dark blue to gem green
On the horizon far out scene

On the edge we play
Never to venture far away
The attraction is primitive
In it lies our heritage

Once having lived with it
One cannot live without it
The sounds of the swells
In our souls dwell

WEDGEPORT – Bill Boudreau
~ Poems, Folklore, History, Images ~

L'Hetriere

L'Hetriere, a child's fantasy grandeur
As little boy, my sanctuary
A place to get away and wander
And satisfy my spirit of adventure

Marsh interrupted by wooded hills
Narrow path from mainland
Thick with ash trees and frills
Walking with stick in hand

Young mind's imagination soaring
Serpents, dragons, and I ready to flee
Sensing a tall dark shadow following
Trees like giants towered over me

On the far side I would reach the sea
Pretend I'd found the edge of the world
Sea birds, other lands as far as I could see
Distant islands, clouds in twirl

Searching for a castle or treasure
Forgotten, lost by an ancient culture
The idea that this could be
Was so very real to me

Now that I'm away and grown
When I go back and visit my home
I go and venture in the *Hetriere*
And then, I become a little boy again!

Acadians

Acadians, Acadians,
Who are we?
Acadians, Acadians,
Who are we?

Are we a mythical people?
From a mythical land
Long ago lost in antiquity
In search of an identity

With suffering and toil
Acadia's spirit is in our souls
Acadia's fire is in our hearts
This land long ago torn apart

Scattered in the world
Returned and began anew
In the sea we've found our pearl
Guided by a gold star in the blue

We are Acadians
We hear a voice from afar
In time and space
We know who we are!

WEDGEPORT – Bill Boudreau
~ Poems, Folklore, History, Images ~

(Painting by Thomas Davies, 1758)

1755 (a song – English version)

Refrain:
In a land long ago
Where the tide runs so low
A village set aflame
Soldiers with no shame

With toil and faith we lived
Love of peace and family
God our only beacon
English Crown our enemy

(Refrain)

In seventeen fifty-five
In ships sent far away
Returned home to find
Our villages given away

WEDGEPORT – Bill Boudreau
~ Poems, Folklore, History, Images ~

Today we live in pride
We've emerged in many lands
We share a unified vision
Evangeline holds our hands

(Refrain)

1755 (a song – French version)

Refrain:

Un pays de longtemps
Où la mer coule haut
Des villages mit en fer
Soldier avec pas de honte

Avec trivail et foi on na vie
Amor de paix et famille
Dieu état notre compass
Couronne Englais notre ennemi

(Refrain)

Dans 17-cent ciaquante-cinq
Force dans des bateaus
Retourner a notre pays
Nos villages état donné

(Refrain)

Maitanant on vie fier
Dans beaucoup de pays
On na la méme vue
Évangéline tient notre mains

WEDGEPORT – Bill Boudreau
~ Poems, Folklore, History, Images ~

WEDGEPORT – Bill Boudreau
~ Poems, Folklore, History, Images ~

~ Images ~

Off to Conquer the Atlantic Ocean

Marais – Canals

WEDGEPORT – Bill Boudreau
~ Poems, Folklore, History, Images ~

Sun and Fog embrace Saint Michael church

A clear day in Wedgeport

WEDGEPORT – Bill Boudreau
~ Poems, Folklore, History, Images ~

Fruits de Mer

WEDGEPORT – Bill Boudreau
~ Poems, Folklore, History, Images ~

Repose

Ready for the Deep

Tusket Islands

St. Marton Island looking toward Harris Island

WEDGEPORT – Bill Boudreau
~ Poems, Folklore, History, Images ~

Deep Cove

Pussy Willow

WEDGEPORT – Bill Boudreau
~ Poems, Folklore, History, Images ~

Scallop Haul

Jules Pothier's, Pierre Boudreau's Houses, and Wedgeport Inn
Painting by Willie LeBlanc

Big Halibut

Close Up

WEDGEPORT – Bill Boudreau
~ Poems, Folklore, History, Images ~

Herring Load

Tuna Wharf Museum

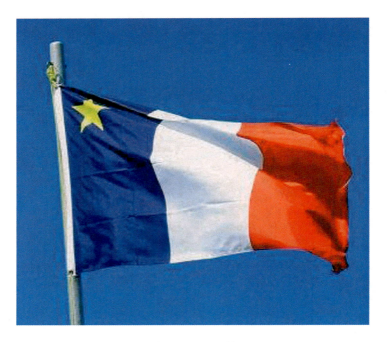

Vive L'Acadie

WEDGEPORT – Bill Boudreau
~ Poems, Folklore, History, Images ~

Expulsion – a 1755 Tragedy
Bill Boudreau – www.billboudreau.com

(A version of this article/prose will appear in my upcoming book, Beyond Acadia)

Spring 1955, throughout southwest Nova Scotia, Acadian villages had begun to prepare for the summer festival highlighting the 200th anniversary of the Acadian's expulsion by the British Crown.

Wedgeport, my village, citizen activities exploded. Men, women, and students built replicas of early settlers' implements: canoes, boats, fishing gears, hand crafted farm and home tools, dancing stages, and flatbed floats. Women stitched early 18th century costumes. Every house flew the Acadian flag—blue, white, red, with a gold star in the blue.

WEDGEPORT – Bill Boudreau
~ Poems, Folklore, History, Images ~

The week before the festival I visited my grandparents Boudreau, the place where I was born on the Cape Road. Grandma had always fascinated me with stories of the past. In her late 70s, her mind remained vibrant.

I entered the house. "Hello! Grandma."

"Billy!"

She sat in her usual rocker by the front window that faced the road. "Smells good." I kissed her on the cheek.

"What's cooking?"

"Haven't seen you in quite a while." She reached, took my hands, and looked me over. "Where have you been? You're getting thinner. You eat well? You hungry?"

"I eat well and a bit hungry Where's Grandpa?"

"Gone to the store. Morning visits with his friends. Talk old times. Drink coffee. Sit over there, Billy." She pointed at her husband's chair. "Tell me about yourself. Is it true what I hear about you and a girl?"

"It is."

"Andrew á Charlie's daughter, right?"

"Yeah."

"Don't think I know her—Might have seen her at church."

"I'm sure you did." I studied Grandma's face. She had more lines than the last time I saw her.

WEDGEPORT – Bill Boudreau
~ Poems, Folklore, History, Images ~

"You should come and see us more often."

"I'll try."

"Bring the girl—we'd like to meet her." She adjusted her seating that crowded the sides. The rocker squeaked. "What's her name?"

"Dorothy."

She looked out the window. "My eyes are not what they used to be."

Grandma Boudreau must have been a very pretty woman in her youth. Now her face wore deep folds. She had endured rural life, living off the land. Her eyes were still alive and quick. She kept herself well groomed. Her gray hair pulled back tight and rolled in a bun, dignified. She made good use of her seventh grade education: wrote letters to relatives in Boston, read the newspaper, church bulletins, and letters to Grandpa who was illiterate.

She heaved herself up, pulled down on her blue, white polka-dotted dress, adjusted her white apron, and wobbled to the stove. She checked the pots, added a little water from the kettle, came and sat down again. "We have a big celebration coming."

"Yes, to honor our heritage—it must have been a terrible time," I said.

Silent for a few moments, she said, "Billy, my grandmother told me stories of her grandmother, Dauphine, who was expelled from Acadia. She was only a child at the time." She looked out the window and dabbed her eyes under her glasses. "A time of great suffering for our people. The deportation started in October 1755 in Grand Pre and spread to surrounding villages—expulsion on a grand scale. The English had sailed in the Bay of Fundy and anchored offshore. The leader of the army summoned the Acadian men in the church at Grand Pre. The British Crown had told them they were going to be given land. It was a trick. Once in the small sanctuary, they became prisoners. Soldiers with guns and bayonets surrounded them. The word came that the Acadians would be exiled to other countries. Acadia, our ancestors' home and beautiful land, cultivated that took over 150 years—taken."

She wiped her eyes. "Our ancestors were a gentle people, Billy. Did not believe in war. Just wanted to be left alone. Live in peace with their families. Faith in God.

"We heard of the atrocities. On that day," she said, "and some time after, our people, guiltless, herded like cattle on old frigates. Sent away to strange places." She continued to gaze through the window, her only view of the outside world. "Their goods taken away. Strength of their bodies determined the amount they could keep. Separation of wives and husbands. Old folks from families. The English Crown wanted to destroy the Acadian culture, forever."

She went on to tell me that her great, great grandmother, Dauphine, and her mother were separated from her father, Jacob, just before loading on a ship. Dauphine witnessed her older brother, Julian, 18, hit in the head with the butt of a rifle as he attempted to stop the breakup of the family. They dragged him away, unconscious. No family member ever saw him again.

Grandma stood, limping on her right leg, she went to the stove and peered inside the pots, moved one aside, picked up a log from a box behind the stove, lifted the cast iron cover, and shoved the chunk of wood in the fire. She sprinkled a few lumps of coal using a small shovel from a bucket on the floor then grabbed a poker, stoked the flames. She moved the pots back. Wiped her hands on her apron, shuffled to her chair, fell in. The rocker squeaked.

"Acadians endured a torturous time," she said. "Dauphine and her family waited on the coast for their turn to be loaded. Cold wet fog hung low on the village. Shivering, Dauphine cuddled to her mother. They could see the ships' silhouettes offshore, like dragons waiting for victims. Dauphine said that throughout her life, not a day had gone by without thinking of the cruelty. She cried silently. Soldiers screamed orders, shot guns in the air to maintain order. In resignation, the old folks obeyed. A few young men attempted to rebel, outnumbered, the British crushed them—knocked them down, stabbed, shot as they ran. The soldiers executed their orders with precision, no escape allowed. Get the Acadians out of Acadia. That was the British Crown's edict."

She stopped rocking and remained silent for a moment. Then she said, "The dispersion went on and with each day the hardship increased. Food became scarce. Old people who could not endure the trauma died on the shore, buried there without markers. The great tide of the Bay of Fundy washed their remains into the vast Atlantic Ocean.

"Temporary camps on the flats provided for those who waited," she said. "Once on board, the ships sailed out of the Bay of Fundy. In the mornings, more ships waited offshore. The cycle repeated until no Acadian stood on our beautiful land."

My body tensed as her story unfolded. My wet palms fisted. I breathed deep. The cooking food odor distracted my thoughts.

Her voice trembled. "From the decks they saw their possessions, their homes, barns, chicken houses, and cultivated fields put to flame. Soldiers killed the farm animals. Those not needed for food were thrown in wells to rot and poison the water. Settlements that took more than 100 years to develop—destroyed. As I said, the very young, the old, and the sick that could not stand the cold, lack of proper nourishment, and the dampness, died, buried on the mud flats. Dauphine saw many kneel where love ones lay in the soft marsh. At bayonet point, soldiers pushed the grievers away, marched them to dories, and rowed the defenseless to the ships.

"Evenings on shores by bonfires, the Acadians gathered, consoled each other."

Grandma pushed her glasses up and dried her eyes, again.

"The Acadians had heard that the French from Quebec would come in their defense. They never came. Of course, they prayed to God, and sought guidance from the priest among them."

This time she pulled her spectacles off and with the corner of her apron, wiped the lenses.

"The guards camped on shore not far from the Acadians. At night the soldiers amused themselves. By the light of lanterns and bonfires, the English played cards, drank liquor, laughed, and partied all night. Not uncommon for soldiers to take Acadian women, bring them to their tents for the night, rape them while parents, husbands watched and listened, helplessly. Monsters! The English who wrote Canadian history, trivialized and clouded the actual horrible events."

"It's only through someone like you, Grandma, that we learn the truth."

History told that the Acadians' were expelled to far off places: the 13 colonies along the American coast and as far south as Louisiana, Belle Isle, an island on the northwest coast of France, England, the Falkland Islands, and the Caribbean Islands. After the dispersion, British immigrants took the Acadian's land. At the time of the American Revolution, many British Crown loyalists left the colonies and established themselves in Acadia. A number of years later, the Acadians were permitted to return. Those who did established villages along the southwest coast of Nova Scotia.

"It must have felt hopeless on those ships in the Atlantic, late fall," I said.

Grandma continued talking as if she had experienced the tragedy herself. "Some trips were several weeks long, others months. Many died along the way. Yes, the Atlantic Ocean is violent, merciless. The burial of the dead were devoid of proper rituals. The priest gave the last rites, bodies dumped in the ocean."

She paused, looked toward the stove and returned her gaze at the window. "The crewmen on those ships were the scum of English society. Many were criminals, drunks, vagabonds, and treated the human cargo harshly. Sanitation not fit for animals. They trampled on each other and human waste. Think of the stench and smell of death. Clustered in hulls—the sick, old, and children. Human shivers, scent of fever, smell of excrements, moans of the old folks wanting the end to come—whimpers of babies. Doom echoed in the cracklings of the vessel's frame and faded into the cold ocean wind."

She repositioned herself. "My back's been bothering me," she said and rubbed her side.

"Grandma, when was the last time you saw doctor?"

She ignored my question. "From the crew's living quarters, at night the Acadians heard laughter and shouts. The soldiers partied until the early hours of the morning. Then silence in the darkness, except for the ocean slapping the ship, waves twisting the frame that creaked as the vessel jerked, bounced on the ocean. Groans, moans, last gasps before death. My grandmother had been told that it was common, in the mornings, for the crew to come in the hull, dragged the dead like bags of potatoes, throw them overboard."

Grandma got up again. "Better get the pork chops in the oven. Grandpa will be here soon." She went into the pantry. "I've put extras for you, Billy. Hope you like them." She pushed the pan in the oven.

"Anything you cook, I love."

She sat down, peered closer to the window. "I see Grandpa coming."

WEDGEPORT – Bill Boudreau
~ Poems, Folklore, History, Images ~

About the Author

Bill Boudreau was born, and grew up, in Wedgeport. He's the author of *Olsegon: Wolfwood Forest and Massacre Island*, a Nova Scotia two-mystery (Wedgeport setting and landscape) novel, *Disharmony in Paradise, a* novella, and *Moments in Time*, a short-story collection. These books are available on Amazon.com and Kindle. *Olsegon* received a favorable review in the Oklahoma Gazette, Nov. 1st, 2006 issue. *Massacre Island* won second place in the Central Oklahoma Roundtable of Authors, C.O.R.A.'s 2005 Contest. The Oklahoma City *Seasoned Reader* published Bill's short-short personal story, First Confession, in the Oct. 2007 issue. The *LLI* (Longlife Learning Institute) Review published, a personal story, "Interlude" in the September 2011 issue. NPR's This I Believe published his essay "Character" in November 2011. In April, 2012, Bill published his novel *Redemption Island* (the story takes the reader to Chebec, a former name for Wedgeport) and it's available on Amazon.com and Kindle. Currently, Bill is working on the final draft of a creative-nonfiction book, Beyond Acadia.

Visit Bill's website: www.billboudreau.com

Made in the USA
Monee, IL
17 April 2021